DEC 2 8 2015

WITHDRAWN

D1000007

X
2018

ESSENTIAL SEWING BASICS
for babies and children

ESSENTIAL SEWING BASICS
for babies and children

Jenny Benjamin

First published in 2014 by New Holland Publishers Pty Ltd
London • Sydney • Auckland

The Chandlery Unit 114 50 Westminster Bridge Road London SE1 7QY United Kingdom
1/66 Gibbes Street Chatswood NSW 2067 Australia
218 Lake Road Northcote Auckland New Zealand

www.newhollandpublishers.com

Copyright © 2014 New Holland Publishers Pty Ltd
Copyright © 2014 in text: Jenny Benjamin
Copyright © 2014 in images: Sue Stubbs

All rights reserved. No part of this publication may be reproduced, stored in a retrieval system or transmitted, in any form or by any means, electronic, mechanical, photocopying, recording or otherwise, without the prior written permission of the publishers and copyright holders.

A record of this book is held at the British Library and the National Library of Australia.

ISBN 9781742575179

Managing Director: Fiona Schultz
Project Editor: Simona Hill
Designer: Caryanne Cleevely
Photographs: Sue Stubbs
Proofreader: Vicky Fisher
Production Director: Olga Dementiev
Printer: Toppan Leefung Printing Ltd (China)

10 9 8 7 6 5 4 3 2 1

Keep up with New Holland Publishers on Facebook
www.facebook.com/NewHollandPublishers

Contents

3 0053
01083
2940

Introduction

I am absolutely hooked on fabric. I love the endless possibilities for creating things it offers with its vast array of textures, colours and patterns, and I love the way fabrics can make me feel. Almost every day I create something with fabric, whether it's a cushion, dress or quilt. There are so many combinations of colours and patterns that each day often feels like an endless fabric adventure. Some days I choose calming greens and aquas. Other days I feel the need to brighten my spirit with the warmth of reds and oranges. At other times my curiosity leads me to combine new colours and patterns. Some work and some don't, but I always have fun experimenting.

What I choose to make depends on a few factors: my mood, the time I have available and sometimes the weather. I enjoy machine-sewing and hand-stitching, as well as decorating fabric by stamping and printing with fabric inks. I make clothes, cushions, tablecloths, napkins, peg bags and even doorstops. Lately, I've rediscovered my love of wool in learning to crochet and in picking up some knitting needles again.

I've been surrounded by colour from as far back as I can remember. My family ran a paint shop and during my school and university years I often helped out, and enjoyed assisting customers, select paint colours. My love of colour is now reflected in the selection of fabrics that I choose to make clothes and homewares for my Pipstars label.

My life changed quite dramatically when I had my children. No longer working, I had more time to do creative things, and to make unique and special things for my daughters. I started hand-stitching and then machine sewing. The more projects I tried the more I wanted to create and I discovered that I had a talent for making things. Soon I started to tweak project patterns, adapting them to my style and tastes.

I believe we can all sew and make things, whether it's for someone we love or for ourselves. Having children to make things for provided a huge motivation for me to sew.

Now, through my Pipstars label and shop I have so many people to make things for, and with whom I can share the joy of unique and handmade items.

In this book I wanted the projects to be something that anyone could complete, even if they have never sewn or made anything before. Making things is great fun and to see your creations bringing joy to someone you love is so satisfying.

I like to design items that can be made quickly and put to use straight away. My style is contemporary, simple and colourful. I don't follow rules and love to mix fabrics and colours, to have fun with everything I make. Practical and useful items appeal to me such as clothes, bags, cushions, and so on. I want quick results so that I can move on to something new and fresh.

If you are a beginner I encourage you to have a go without putting pressure on yourself to achieve perfection. Chances are the first time you make a project you may not be completely happy with the result.

Think of the first one as practice and know that you will improve as you keep making things. Choose a simple project from the book for your first item. Build your confidence. So many of these projects are basically made by sewing straight lines. You can do all these projects easily if you take it slowly, read the instructions and work step by step. And remember to enjoy the process.

Sewing Basics

Sewing Basics

You may know some of this information and terminology already, but refreshing your memory will keep the knowledge fresh and you may learn some new terms and techniques that will help make your sewing a success. All the patterns are in the envelope at the back of the book.

Fabric Grain

All woven fabrics have a straight grain, which runs parallel to the selvages (the fabric edges that do not fray). The lengthwise threads are the warp and the crosswise threads are the weft. When positioning pattern pieces on fabric it is important to find the straight grain so the pieces you cut from the fabric will hang straight and not twist.

Measurements

Measurements are provided in metric with imperial in brackets. Choose one or the other and stick to it. Don't alternate between the two.

Seam Allowance

This is the width of fabric allowed for stitching the seams. The range of seam allowance widths varies from 5–20 mm (¼–¾ in) depending on the project. More experienced sewers can sew with accuracy and manage smaller seam allowances. The less experienced sewer will probably feel more comfortable with a generous seam allowance. Patterns will state if any seam allowance is included or if you need to add a seam allowance when cutting out the fabric. Read the patterns and instructions carefully to check the seam allowances. Be careful not to change seam allowances since this will alter the size of the finished item.

Bias Binding

Bias binding can be bought ready-made at fabric shops, though you can make it from any fabric. Narrow fabric strips are cut at a 45-degree angle to the fabric grain and then joined together, to create maximum

stretch in the fabric. Bias binding can be used to enclose curved edges such as armholes because the fabric has some stretch, as well as straight edges where it will lie flat. You can make your own bias binding by cutting strips, joining them together and folding and pressing the raw edges inwards.

Threads

Always use the same thread in the bobbin and through the needle of a sewing machine. The manual for your machine should include a thread guide. Polyester thread is recommended for general sewing.

It is best to co-ordinate the thread colour with the fabric. Working with a contrast thread colour can give an original look to your sewing; however, if your seams are a little wonky they will stand out more.

For embroidery, use embroidery cottons, which have multiple strands of thread that can be separated depending on the project.

Fabrics

I prefer to use cotton fabrics when making things for kids, because they come in different weights.

Lawn cotton or voile is fine and light but often too delicate for items that are subject to the level of wear and tear and tough treatment that children can inflict.

Quilting cotton is lightweight and suitable for clothing and some decorative items.

Cotton drill is a medium-weight fabric ideal for boys' shorts, cushion covers and tote bags.

Canvas is heavier and useful for floor cushions or bags, but probably too stiff for clothing.

Generally it's inadvisable to mix fabrics of different weights in a project. However, you may decide to use quilting cotton for a cushion front and cotton drill for the back. As a guide I would recommend you stick to the same weight of fabric in one project, unless stated otherwise.

Fabric colour and pattern are very personal choices. You may like to choose fabric according to your child's favourite colour, or there may be something in their wardrobe or room that you would like to match.

Fabrics with different designs can be mixed with fabulous results. You can mix spots with stripes, or petite florals with geometric designs.

Stick to a palette of two or three colours that work together. Arrange the fabrics next to each other and see how they look in different combinations.

You could choose a monochromatic colour theme and mix designs only, choosing tone-on-tone fabrics in the colour. For example select three or four fabrics in tones of pink, with a spot, a petite floral, a stripe and a larger pink patterned design. Put the fabrics together and they make a striking effect, all in tones of pink. You can work with complementary or contrasting colours. Let your creative spirit free and play around with fabric

It is important to think about the pattern on fabrics when selecting them for a project. Some designs are 'one way' patterns so the design is repeated in the same direction along the fabric

length. This means that you cannot spin pattern pieces around or you would cut the design upside down. A 'two-way' pattern, or all-over design, can be turned around 180 degrees and the design will look exactly the same. Working with an all-over design means you can get more out of the fabric with less wastage.

Keep any fabric scraps and offcuts. There are always uses for bits and pieces. Maybe an offcut could be used to make an appliqué motif on a baby singlet, or you could patch offcuts together to make the front of a cushion cover. Leftover pieces could be used to add decoration to a laundry bag. If space allows, it is good to sort scraps into colour groups, so when you need a specific colour of fabric in a hurry you can quickly find what you need.

In quilting and fabric shops you may hear the term 'fat quarter' and wonder what that means. A fat quarter is the piece of fabric made by cutting a metre (or yard) of fabric off a bolt of quilting fabric (114 cm/44 in wide), then cutting it in half vertically and then in half again horizontally. It measures

approximately 50 x 57 cm (20 x 22½ in). This is often a more useful shape to purchase than a long narrow strip cut off the end of a bolt. Most quilting shops have a minimum quantity that they will sell, usually 20 cm (8 in), giving a piece of fabric 20 x 114 cm (8 x 44 in). You can see that, at times, a fat quarter would be more useful.

Seams

Pinning Seams

Place the two pieces of fabric to be joined right sides together, lining up the edges. Insert pins at right angles to the fabric edge, spacing them evenly. As you sew the seam remove the pins.

Sewing Straight Seams

Place the fabrics right sides together matching the raw edges and pin the seam. Noting the seam allowance given in the pattern, sew a few stitches to start the seam, then back stitch a few stitches to secure the stitching, and continue along the seam with straight stitch, removing the pins as you sew. At the end of the seam make a few back stitches to secure the seam. Remove the pins, then press the seam flat, with an iron, on the wrong side of the fabric.

Sewing a Right-Angle Corner

Sew to within a seam-allowance' width of the end of the seam, and finish with the needle down in the fabric. Raise the presser foot, rotate the fabric 90 degrees, lower the presser foot and continue sewing.

Sewing Curved Seams

To make sure a convex seam (one that curves outward) sits flat, clip around the curve at regular intervals up to 1 or 2 mm ($^1/16$ in) from the stitched seam. Clip too close and you are at risk of cutting the seam stitching.

For a concave seam (one that curves inward) cut small v-shaped notches at regular intervals around the curve. Stitch along the seam line, press the seam with an iron and turn right side out. Press again. You can topstitch 2 mm ($^1/16$ in) from the edge to ensure the curve stays flat.

If you lack confidence, you can draw the line with a fading marker and follow the marked line with the machine needle when you sew the curve.

Making French Seams

Place the fabrics wrong sides together with raw edges matching. Pin, then machine-sew a seam 1 cm ($^3/8$ in) in from the edge of the fabrics. Trim the seam allowance to 3 mm ($^1/8$ in) from the seam. Fold the fabric right sides together and stitch another seam 5 mm (¼ in) from the edge. The raw edges of the fabric are encased inside the seam. This is a super neat finish that works on fine fabrics, quilting cottons and medium-weight decorative fabrics.

Trimming Corners

To reduce the bulk at right-angle corners diagonally trim off the corner fabric before turning the item right side out. Useful when making cushions or bags.

Machine Stitches

Straight Stitch

The most frequently used stitch on a sewing machine is the straight stitch. The length of the stitch determines the strength of the seam and can be adjusted on the machine. Generally on fine fabrics a shorter stitch is used for strength and on thick (therefore strong) fabrics a longer stitch is used. A straight stitch set at maximum length is used for basting (tacking) so it is easier to unpick the seams later.

Zigzag Stitch

Many projects in this book call for the cut edge of the fabric to be zigzag stitched to prevent the fabric from fraying. The length and width of the stitches should be adjusted according to the type of fabric. Generally, use short stitches set close together for fine fabrics, and longer and more open stitches for thick fabrics. An overlocker does a wonderful edge stitching while trimming excess fabric, so if you have access to an overlocker please make use of it. Otherwise the zigzag stitch will do the job just fine.

Topstitching

Topstitching is a straight stitch sewn on the right side of the fabric usually made with a sewing machine, either as a single or double row of stitching. It can be decorative or to strengthen a seam.

Basting (Tacking)

Basting is temporary stitching to hold pieces of fabric together until the final stitching is completed. To baste with a sewing machine set the straight stitch to the maximum length and sew just outside the line of the final seam and leave the thread ends unfinished.

Using a bright-coloured thread makes stitches easier to see for unpicking later. Basting can also be done by hand, though this is more time consuming.

Hand Stitches

Blanket Stitch

Start from the back of the work, bring the needle through to the front of the fabric and close to the raw edge. Take the needle down into the fabric from right side to wrong side, a short distance away from the point where the needle first emerged. Bring the needle through the loop and pull tight. For the next stitch, move along and take the needle from the front to the back of the work, as before, pulling the thread through but leaving a loop, then the needle goes through the loop and you pull the thread all the way through. Continue on around the edges, spacing out the stitches evenly and making the stitches the same length.

When you return to the starting point, take the needle through tthe original loop, then to the back of the work and tie off with the beginning thread. The spacing of the stitches gives quite a different effect. This stitch can be used to edge fabrics or as an outline for a design.

Chain Stitch

Make a knot in the end of your thread. Bring the needle from the back to the front of the fabric. Hold the thread with your thumb against the front of the fabric close to the needle so the thread makes a loop. Insert the needle down through the fabric very close to where the thread came through, then bring it up a stitch length away. Make sure the loop is outside or under the needle as you pull the thread through the fabric. For the next stitch take the needle from the front to the back of the fabric through the first loop chain stitch, then bring it up a short gap ahead, holding the thread against the fabric with your thumb to ensure the loop is outside or under the needle. Repeat the process to make the next link in the chain. To complete the chain simply secure the last loop with a tiny straight stitch.

Slip Stitch

This is a 'hidden' stitch often used to close openings in seams and hand-stitch hems. The fabric fold of the

seam provides somewhere to hide the stitches. Start by knotting the end of your thread then take the needle behind the fold and pull the thread through the crease of the fold to the front. Pick up a few threads from the opposite fabric then take the needle back through the fold of the fabric and come out further along the fold.

Running Stitch

This is a very easy hand stitch, basically taking the thread in and out of the fabric keeping the length of the stitch and the gap between stitches even. Running stitch is worked in a line.

Equipment

Sewing Machine

A basic sewing machine is all you need to make the projects in this book. Every project requires just two machine stitches – straight stitch and zigzag stitch. All basic sewing machine models manufactured now offer these stitches as standard. The manufacturer's instruction manual will explain how to thread the machine, load bobbins, change the sewing foot and alter the stitch tension.

If you are new to machine-sewing take some time to practise on scrap fabric. On a double thickness of fabric draw parallel lines and sew over them with the sewing machine needle. Use a bright-coloured thread so you can easily see the stitches. Start with some straight stitches, sew to the end and reverse-stitch a little way to secure the seam. Adjust the length of the stitches to see the effect of the different lengths. Draw curved lines and practise sewing curves. The handwheel on the sewing machine can be turned manually to slowly stitch something tricky. If you find it difficult to sew very slowly with the foot control, try sewing by manually turning the hand wheel.

Sewing machine needles come in a variety of sizes for using on different weight fabrics. They blunt with use, so change them every now and then to get better results.

Scissors

Cutting paper with scissors dulls the blades so keep a pair of household scissors especially for cutting paper. Buy a quality pair of fabric scissors with blades about 20–25 cm (8–10 in) long and reserve them for cutting fabric only. Have another small pair for trimming threads or making small cuts in awkward places.

Pins

Buy some quality dressmaker's pins, which are fine and will not make holes in your fabrics. If you buy pins with little plastic heads they may melt when you iron over them, so I recommend buying pins with a glass head. They won't melt and are easy to see both in the fabric and when you drop them on the floor.

Appliqué Paper

Appliqué paper (fusible webbing) is used to apply decorative fabric motifs to another fabric. This double-sided adhesive product has one smooth paper side on which you draw the motif and one grainy (glue) side. Draw the motif on the paper side of the product, making sure that you draw the mirror image of the motif that you want. Cut out the motif slightly larger than the drawn shape, allowing a small margin all around. Iron the shape, grainy side down, to the wrong side of the fabric. Protect the iron and the ironing board by using baking paper under and on top of the motif and fabric.

Once it has adhered, trim the motif to the drawn lines and remove the layer of backing paper to reveal a thin layer of glue. Place the motif glue-side down on the right side of the fabric to which it is to be applied and iron, or fuse, in place.

Tape Measure

You will use a tape measure constantly. Buy a simple loose tape measure or a retractable one. A clear plastic 30 cm (12 in) stationery rule is also handy for quick measuring.

Templates

Templates are used to make shapes similar to a pattern. Templates made from light card stock are very robust and can be used over and over again to trace around onto fabric using a marker pen (that can fade or be washed out), or onto appliqué paper using a pen or pencil. You can use a template to make a paper pattern, which can then be pinned onto fabric and cut around. Then, if the paper is damaged when cutting around the paper pattern you can use the template to make a new pattern.

Seam Ripper

A seam ripper is a useful tool for quickly cutting basting threads or unpicking a mistake. Most sewing machines have one in the tool box.

Fabric Markers

Chalk was the traditional tool to mark fabric for sewing but new fabric marking pens make the job easier.

Marking pens come in different types – wash away or fade away. Having one in your sewing kit is essential. Test the pen on a corner of your fabric before using to mark out a pattern.

Hand-Sewing Needles

Have an assortment of hand-sewing needles for various tasks, such as closing seams, embroidery and sewing on buttons or hand-basting. The needle should be about 4 cm (1½ in) long.

Grid Rule

Grid-marked transparent quilter's rules can be handy for marking seam allowances or making simple patterns. It's not essential but is very useful.

Tracing Paper

Buy large sheets of tracing paper from a fabric shop for tracing the patterns in this book. Using small sheets and trying to join them can be tricky.

In the Bedroom

Fabric Hearts

You will need

1 or 2 fabrics for the heart, each measuring 12 cm (4¾ in) wide x 15 cm (6 in) high

Heart template

Ribbon, 42 cm (16½ in) long, for the hanging loop

Co-ordinating thread

Polyester toy stuffing

These sweet little hearts are so simple to make and a lovely gift for someone special. I made one for my daughter when she started school. She popped it in her pocket, then when she felt the need for some comfort she slipped her hand inside her pocket and touched the heart. It worked a treat. So well, in fact, I had to make one for her best friend because apparently she was feeling sad too!

Small offcuts and scraps are ideal to use in the combinations of fabrics and ribbons. You can make hearts with different fabrics on each side, or the same fabric on both sides. They look great hanging from a door knob or pinned to a message board. The ribbon hanging loop could be made a different length.

The template for this project is on page 122.

1 To cut out the fabric hearts, place the fabric for the back of the heart right side up on the work surface. Place the fabric for the heart front right side down on top. Pin the template to both fabrics and cut out.

2 Fold the hanging loop ribbon in half and place it between the front and back heart fabrics with the cut ends at the top and the loop at the bottom. Pin in place at the top of the heart, leaving 1 cm (3/8 in) of ribbon protruding at the edge.

3 Pin the fabrics together, leaving a 3–4 cm (1½–1¾ in) opening at one side of the lower part of the heart, as marked on the template. The loop of ribbon should come out of the opening.

4 Starting at the bottom of the opening, machine-sew around the heart, leaving a 1 cm (3/8 in) seam allowance. When you get to the top take care to catch the ribbon in the seam. Use a smaller machine stitch to sew across the ribbon to make it extra secure, if you like.

5 Trim any excess fabric from the seams, then turn the heart right side out. Use the point of your scissors to carefully push out the point at the bottom of the heart.

6 Pack the heart firmly with stuffing. Too little stuffing and it won't have a nice shape, but too much can look odd.

7 Hand-stitch the seam closed.

Simple Cushion Cover

You will need

Heart template (see p. 122)

4 squares of fabric,
19 x 19 cm (7½ x 7½ in)

1 front lining,
35 x 35 cm (13¾ x 13¾ in)

2 pieces for the back,
27.5 x 35 cm (10¾ x 13¾ in)

35 cm (13¾ in) square cushion insert

Co-ordinating thread

When I first started sewing I was terrified of putting in a zipper and instead limited my sewing projects to things I could make without one. These cushion covers are designed and made with this in mind, utilising an envelope opening method so that the cover can be removed for washing. They're also another way to use up scraps of fabric. I cut four squares from four fabrics and sew them together to make the cushion front.

I To make the cushion back pieces, turn in a 5 mm (¼ in) seam along one long edge of each piece and, using an iron, press in place. Turn in another 5 mm (¼ in) along the same edge and pin. Stitch in place using straight stitch. Set aside.

2 To make the cushion front, press the four squares and work out the placement. Pin the left side pieces, right sides together, then stitch one edge, allowing a 1.5 cm (½ in) seam allowance. Repeat with the other side. Press the seams towards the darker fabric side. Pin the two rectangles together with right sides facing and matching centre seams. Sew together to make one panel. Trim any threads.

3 Place the front panel right side down and centre the lining fabric on top. Pin together. Turn the pinned piece, so that the front panel is right side up. Arrange one of the back panels with the sewn edge at the bottom, on top of the front panel, aligning raw edges at the top. Pin the top corners to hold firmly in place. Place the second back panel right

side down, with the sewn edge at the top, and partly overlapping the top back panel, squaring up the corners. Pin the bottom corners, then add extra pins around all the edges.

4 Holding the fabrics with the back fabric on top, start sewing the right-hand side seam, using a 1 cm (3/8 in) seam allowance, and beginning halfway between the top right corner and the sewn edge of the backing fabric. Sew all around the cushion cover.

5 Remove the pins, then set the sewing machine to a zigzag stitch. Zigzag the raw edges. Trim any loose threads and turn the cushion right side out. Push out each corner. Put the insert into the cushion.

HINT
Scale the measurements up or down to make larger or smaller cushions.

Owl

This owl is fun to make with his hand-stitching decorative details. You could easily do all the stitching on a sewing machine, if you prefer. This is a marvellous project to make with an older child; they could do the hand-stitching and you could assist with machine-sewing the front and back pieces together.

You will need

Owl templates (see pp. 124–125)

Fabric, for the owl front and back, 40 x 21 cm (16 x 8½ in)

Fabric, for the face mask, 13 x 6 cm (5½ x 2½ in)

Appliqué paper (fusible webbing)

Felt for the wings, beak and feet

Two buttons, each 20 mm (¾ in) diameter, for the eyes

Stranded embroidery cottons (to co-ordinate or contrast with the fabrics and felt)

Polyester toy stuffing

Co-ordinating thread, for machine sewing

I Using the templates provided, cut 1 owl front and 1 owl back from the fabric.

2 Select a fabric for the face mask. With a pencil, trace the mask template onto appliqué paper. Cut the mask out from the paper, allowing 1 cm ($^3/_8$ in) extra all around. Position the grainy side down on the back of the chosen fabric, fuse in place with a hot iron, then accurately cut out the shape along the pencil line. Set aside to cool. Peel the paper layer away from the sticky web. If you rush this step the paper will pull the sticky layer from the fabric.

3 Place the face mask fabric on the owl front fabric. Rub over with an iron and fuse the mask to the fabric.

4 Select an embroidery thread colour to co-ordinate or contrast with the face mask and cut a length. I like to stitch with three strands of the embroidery cotton, so separate the strands out. Leaving a 5 cm (2 in) tail of thread at the back of the work bring your needle through to the front at the bottom centre of the mask. You will use this

tail to tie off at the end. Blanket stitch all the way around the edge of the mask until you reach the beginning. Take the thread to the back and tie off with the tail of thread you left at the beginning. Try to keep your stitches the same size and evenly spaced.

5 Cut out a felt beak using the template provided. Pin in position, then sew in place using running stitch. Tie off the threads securely.

6 Sew on the button eyes using embroidery thread. Playing around with thread colours can really change the look of the face so you could either match the thread to the button so the sewing is less noticeable or use a contrast thread and make the middle of the button more of a feature.

7 Cut out two felt wings using the template provided. Position the wings on the owl front. Only half of the wing is stitched to the owl front, the rest flaps free. Using running stitch and embroidery cotton, sew the wings in place on the owl front.

8 Cut two felt feet using the template provided. Pin the straight edge of the

felt feet to the bottom edge of the owl, raw edges aligned and pin in place from the back.

9 Arrange the back of the owl right side up on the work surface. Place the owl front right side down on top, aligning raw edges. Tuck the wings in so that they won't be caught in the stitching. Pin the front and back together.

IO Leave a 3–4 cm (1¼–1¾ in) opening behind one of the wings for turning the fabric right side out. This helps hide the seam. Machine-stitch around the edges, allowing a 5 mm (¼ in) seam allowance. If you are a little nervous, the seam allowance can be increased to 1 cm (³⁄₈ in).

II Remove all the pins and trim any excess fabric from the seams. This is important around the ears, since excess fabric around small shapes makes it difficult to turn the shapes through to get a neat finish.

I2 Turn the owl right side out. Use the point of the scissors to push out the ears, then fill with stuffing. Make sure the stuffing is evenly packed.

I3 Hand-stitch the seam closed.

Bunting

You will need

Fabric (enough to make 7 flags):
1 flag requires 1 piece of fabric
23 x 30 cm (9 x 12 in)

Flag template (see p. 123)

2.5 m (2¾ yd) bias binding

Co-ordinating thread

Fabric bunting is easy to make and is a wonderful way to co-ordinate colours in a child's bedroom.

The flags of this bunting are double-sided so that if you want to make a long bunting and string it across a room it looks perfect from each side.

Five, six or seven flags makes a good length to tie across a single bedhead or a narrow window. You may need 30 flags to tie up a bunting diagonally from one corner of a bedroom to another.

When buying fabric to make bunting think about the pattern. If the fabric design is a one-way pattern you will have a lot of wastage as you won't be able to flip the template and cut out flags each way. An all-over pattern fabric is more economical as it will yield more flags. A piece of fabric 23 x 30 cm (9 x 12 in) is big enough to cut two triangles to make one complete flag.

These instructions make a 7-flag bunting. The finished width of 1 flag is 17 cm (6¾ in). Allow at least 60 cm (24 in) of binding at each end for tying the bunting in place.

1 Cut out 14 triangles of fabric using the template provided.

2 Iron the fabric. With right sides together, pin, then stitch the triangles together along the two long edges only, using a straight stitch. Leave a 1 cm (3/8 in) seam allowance.

3 Trim the thread ends and any excess fabric. Cut off the fabric tip seam allowance, taking care not to cut too close to the stitching.

4 Turn the flags right side out. Use the point of your scissors to gently push out the point of each triangle. Press with an iron.

5 The bias binding is folded with one side slightly wider than the other. Position it so that the wider side is below. Measure 60 cm (24 in) of bias binding for the tie. Pin to mark the measurement. Pin the first flag in place next to the 60 cm (24 in) pin marker. Pin the next flag so that the two flags just touch each other. Continue pinning the flags to the binding. Once the flags are in place there should be about 60 cm (24 in) of binding left to tie the bunting.

6 Have the binding and flags in your lap as you sit at the sewing machine. Use a small straight stitch to topstitch 1–2 mm (1/16 in) in from the edge. Start about 2 cm (¾ in) from the end of the binding, do a few stitches, then turn and go back along to the narrow end of the tie, stitch along the edge, then turn again and sew back along the edge of the binding. Sew all the way along the tie and pause when you get to the first flag. Unpin the flag and reposition it so that the raw edges are enclosed inside the fold of the bias binding. Pin in place. When you sew to the edge of the flag, pause with the needle down in the fabric (this ensures the flag won't slip or slide), unpin the next flag and reposition it as before inside the fold of the binding. Once all flags have been secured, continue sewing along the edge of the binding to the end. Back-stitch to secure the stitching.

7 Trim threads and press lightly with a warm iron.

Laundry Sack

A fun way to encourage kids to keep their bedrooms tidy is to have individual laundry sacks. I chose quilting cotton for my sack, using the entire width of the fabric. It's an easy shape to sew, and very quick to make. You can use this method to make a drawstring bag of any size for any purpose by changing the fabric measurements. I have made them to store shoes or other paraphernalia.

You will need

Main fabric, 60 x 114 cm (24 x 44 in)

2.5 m (2¾ yd) cotton cord (or wide grosgrain ribbon)

Co-ordinating thread

Appliqué paper (fusible webbing)

Contrast fabric, for appliqué motif (optional)

I Cut a bag front and bag back from the main fabric, each 60 x 55 cm (24 x 22 in).

2 Overlock or zigzag stitch along the long side edges and one short edge (the bag bottom) of each piece. See the Hint overleaf to personalise the sack with contrast fabric.

3 With wrong side facing, turn over 1 cm (^{3}/$_8$ in) at the top raw edge and press with an iron. Turn over a second time by 3 cm (1¼ in) and press. Repeat for the second piece of fabric. This will become the casing for the cord. Put a pin at the bottom of the second pressed fold to mark the spot. This is where the side seams will begin. Unfold the fabric to keep it out of the way when sewing the side seams.

4 Pin the front and back of the bag right sides together, aligning all edges. The side seams should start from the pin markers at the bottom of the second pressed fold.

5 Stitch the two pieces together, allowing a 1 cm (^{3}/$_8$ in) seam allowance, and beginning at the pin

markers (4 cm/1¾ in down from the raw edge) and stitching around the sides and bottom, finishing neatly at the opposite marker.

6 Press the fabric side seams open with the iron. Turn in the seam allowance at each top side edge of the bag, then re-fold and press the top of the sack over. Pin in place.

7 With the wrong side up, sew along the fold edge about 3 mm (^{1}/$_8$ in) in from the edge. Go all the way around the opening. If you prefer you can do the front and back of the sack in two separate sewing lines if the folded edges don't match up neatly on the side seams. Remember to do a few back stitches at each end of these sewing lines to secure the seams.

8 Turn the sack right side out. Use the point of your scissors to gently push out the corners.

9 Cut the length of cord in half, so you have two lengths, each 1.25 m (49 in). Wrap some tape around the ends of the cord to prevent it from unravelling. Attach a large safety pin to one end of the cord and use it to

feed the cord through from the front left side all the way around the bag. Repeat threading the other length all the way around the bag, but this time starting from the front right side. Knot the ends and push the knot into the casing

HINT

Why not personalise the fabric with decoration before you stitch the sack front and back together. Appliquéing a name or initials to the sack saves arguments about whose sack is whose. Type the name or initials in a large font and print it out. When you are happy with the size, tape the motif to a light source (reverse the image), trace it onto appliqué paper. Iron the appliqué paper to the wrong side of a piece of contrast fabric then cut out. When completely cool, peel the backing paper off the motif, position it on the sack front then fuse in place with an iron. Using the sewing machine, topstitch around the edge of the letter to secure it in place.

In the Bedroom

Contemporary Cot Quilt

I love the idea of making and giving a snuggly cot quilt to friends who have just had a baby. Select two fabrics that work well together, then wash and press the fabrics before sewing to ensure any shrinkage happens before you sew up your quilt.

You will need

2 pieces of quilting fabric, the full fabric width x 124 cm (49 in) long

Co-ordinating thread

Contrast thread for the decorative quilting stitches

Washable batting (wadding) 114 x 124 cm (44 x 49 in)

I Cut the selvages off the fabrics. Trim the batting to the same size as the fabric.

2 Arrange the quilt front fabric right side up on a flat work surface. Arrange the backing fabric right side down on top of the front fabric, aligning raw edges. Centre the batting on top. Pin the three layers securely together.

3 Turn the quilt over so the fabric layers are on top and the batting below, and using a 1.5 cm (½ in) seam allowance, start sewing on one of the shorter sides. Back-stitch a little at the start to secure the stitching. Sew all the way around the quilt, leaving an opening of about 15 cm (6 in) for turning the quilt the right way out.

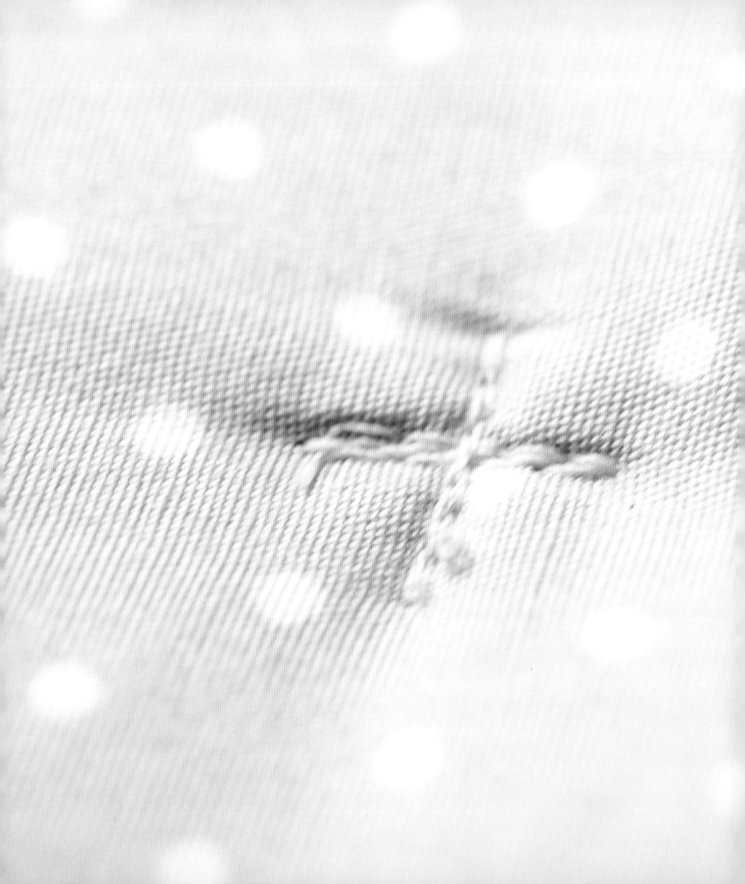

4 Trim the seam allowance from each corner to remove the excess fabric. Turn the quilt the right way out.

5 At the turn-through opening, fold the backing fabric raw edge towards the inside of the quilt, over the batting layer. Smooth across the fabric fold with your fingers. Fold the top layer fabric inside the quilt and finger-press the fabric fold with your fingers. Pin to secure, then hand-sew with an invisible stitch to close the opening.

6 The batting is held firmly in place with stitches, worked in a grid across the surface of the quilt. This can be hand-stitched, but for this project I have provided instructions for using a machine.

7 Arrange the quilt on a flat surface, with the opening (now stitched closed) at the bottom. Mark the first stitching point with a fading marker pen, 8 cm (3¼ in) from the top and side edges. Mark the position of the first row of cross stitches 10 cm (4 in) apart across the width and 8 cm (3¼ in) down from the top edge. Now mark points 10 cm (4 in) below the original marks and continue to mark points down the quilt at 10 cm (4 in) intervals.

8 Set the sewing machine to straight stitch. Each cross stitch is made up of six stitches worked first in one direction, then crossways. Each is overstitched five times in each direction. Do a sample first until you are happy with the result.

9 Once you have sewn each line of the cross, cut the thread and move on to the next marker and repeat until you have stitched over all the markers. This looks fabulous in a contrast colour or bright thread. However, if you are not confident and you want to hide these stitches you could use the co-ordinating threads you used for the seams. Trim all the threads.

Jumbo Floor Cushion

My kids were always taking cushions off the sofa to toss on the floor. They would lie on them while reading or watching television. So I made them some jumbo floor cushions to lie on, roll on, stack up and occasionally to throw at a sibling. They are inexpensive to make, easy to wash and care for, and practical in a busy family home.

You can use lightweight cotton but I recommend something more robust such as a mid-weight cotton or light canvas.

You will need

2 pieces of fabric each 65 x 62 cm (25½ x 24½ in)

Co-ordinating thread

Co-ordinating zipper, 50 cm (20 in) long

65 cm (25½ in) square cushion insert

I To prepare the bottom edge for the zipper, zigzag stitch along one short raw edge of each fabric piece.

2 Place the fabric right sides together, zigzag edges aligned. Measure 5 cm (2 in) down the side from the zigzag edge. This will be the seam allowance. On both the right and left-hand sides draw a line 7 cm (2¾ in) long with a fading marker pen and parallel with the zigzag edges. Stitch along the lines, being sure to back-stitch at the beginning and end to secure the threads. Trim loose

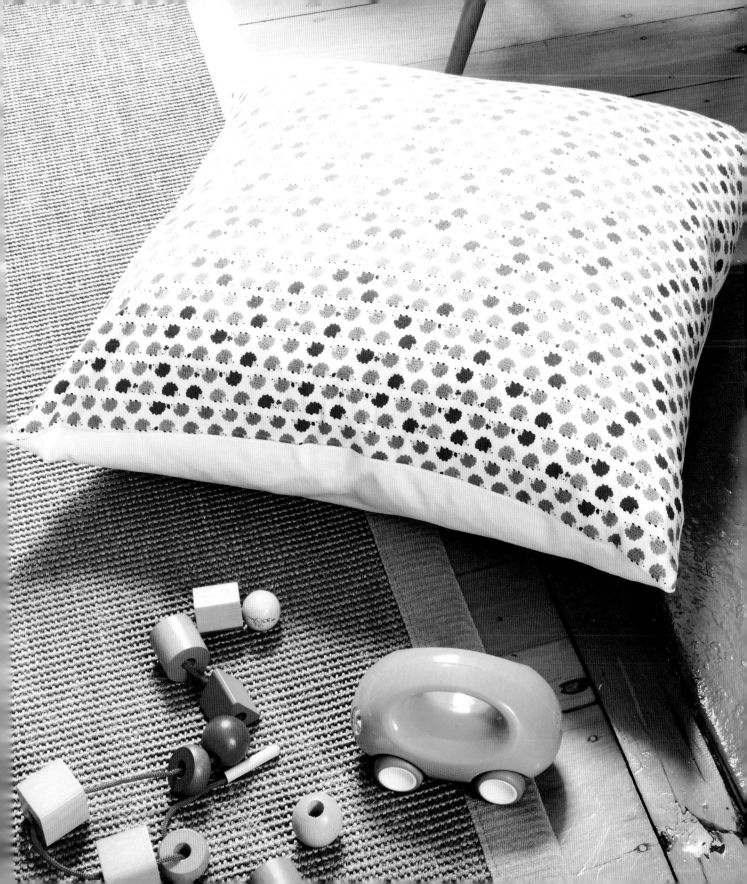

threads. Set the sewing machine to the longest straight stitch and baste between these two seams, leaving a 1 cm (3/8 in) gap between each end of the basting and the start of the stitching. Press the seam open on both sides of the fabric.

3 Open and close the zipper a few times to be sure it works properly. Open out the fabric and place right side down on the work surface. Arrange the zipper right side down between the two stitched lines. Place the zipper teeth just below the folded edge of fabric and the edge of the zipper fabric will be almost flush with the zigzag stitched edge of the cushion fabric and pin in place. Fit the machine's zipper foot and sew along the top side edge of the zipper as close to the teeth as you can, and being sure to keep a straight line. Sew the other side of the zipper, this time not as close to the teeth.

4 Use a seam ripper to unpick the basting stitches to reveal the zipper.

5 With the cushion back and front right sides together, and the zipper open a little way at one end, pin around the cushion using a 15 mm (½ in) seam allowance. Working from the stitched zipper seam, sew down one side, along the bottom and back up the other side. Finish the raw edges with an overlocker or a zigzag stitch.

6 Turn right side out, pushing out the corners. Insert the cushion pad. Smooth out.

In the Wardrobe

In the Wardrobe

Hand–Appliquéd Baby Singlet

I learned to embroider so I could embellish my baby's clothes. I stitched hearts on singlets, ducks on bodysuits and stars on tee-shirts.

You will need

Appliqué templates (see p. 126)

Appliqué paper (fusible webbing)

Garment, to appliqué

Fabric, for appliqué motif

Cotton embroidery thread

I Trace around the template with a pencil on the appliqué paper. Cut out the shape, leaving a margin of 1 cm (3/8 in) all around.

2 Iron the appliqué paper shape to the wrong side of the appliqué fabric. Set aside and allow to cool, then cut out the shape on the drawn line. Peel off the backing paper.

3 Place the garment on the ironing board, position the fabric shape, right side up, and press with an iron to fuse the motif to the garment, taking care not to move the fabric.

4 Cut a length of stranded embroidery cotton and separate three threads out. Leave a 5 cm (2 in) tail of thread and blanket stitch all the way around the shape.

5 Take the thread end through to the back and using the tail you left at the beginning, securely tie off the thread.

Baby Bib

I love to give fabric bibs, which are quick and easy to make, to friends with new babies. You can make classic bibs in soft colours or groovy bibs in bright fabrics for a contemporary look. The pattern for this is in the Wrap Dress pattern in the envelope at the back of the book.

You will need

Cotton fabric, for the bib front

Towelling or other mid-weight fabric, for the bib back

Co-ordinating thread

Press stud

I Using the template, cut out the cotton for the bib front and the towelling for the bib back.

2 Arrange the towelling bib on the work table, right side up. Centre the cotton fabric bib right side down on top. Pin the two layers together, leaving an 8 cm (3¼ in) gap in one straight side (*see template*).

3 Using a 1 cm (³/₈ in) seam allowance, machine-stitch the two layers together, beginning at one side of the marked gap and working around to the other side. Trim the threads and clip the inside neck so it will turn out neatly. Turn the bib right side out.

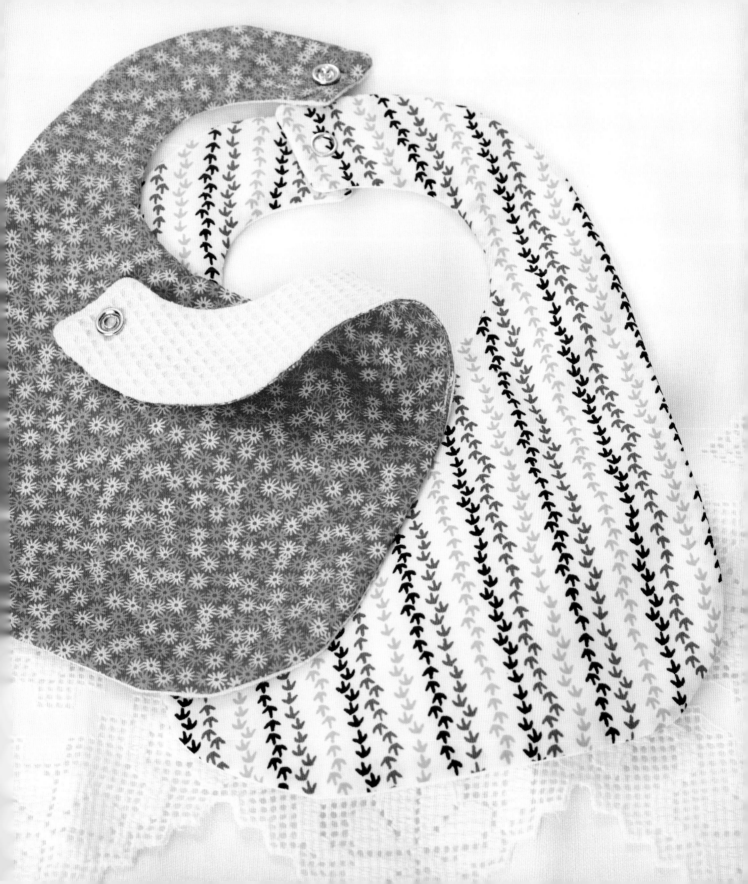

4 At the opening, fold in the seam allowances and press. Topstitch a few millimetres in from the fabric edge to close the gap. Back-stitch at the beginning and end of the stitching to secure the seam, then trim the threads. Fit the stud closure on the back of the bib.

IDEAS

You could make the bib front using two pieces of fabric joined. It is an ideal way to use up smaller pieces of favourite fabrics. Be sure to press the seam open with an iron to give a smooth finish to the front of the bib.

You can easily make a larger bib for an older baby, just increase the neck hole size and make the bib longer. A tee-shirt that is a good fit around the baby's neck will be a good guide for the neck hole opening size.

Twirly Skirt

Skirts that twirl make little girls smile. These instructions are to make a skirt for a 6–8-year-old girl. The fabric tiers are gathered to fit together and the waistband is elasticated. You can adjust the dimensions to make the skirt fit a younger girl by reducing the depth and length of each fabric layer. Trim the selvages off the fabrics.

You will need

Three fabrics, one for each of the 3 tiers

Co-ordinating thread

2 cm (¾ in) wide elastic, for the waist

I Measure the child from the waist to the desired finished length. Divide this number by three to evenly spread the length over the three tiers. This number will be the finished depth of each tier.

2 To the top tier depth add 4 cm (1½ in) for the waistband elastic casing, plus 1.5 cm (½ in) for one seam allowance.

3 To the middle tier and bottom tier depths, add 3 cm (1¼ in) for seam allowances.

4 For the top tier use a full width of fabric, selvage to selvage that measures 114 cm (44 in wide) x the calculated tier depth. For the second tier cut two widths of fabric x the

calculated tier depth. For the bottom tier cut three widths of fabric x the calculated tier depth.

5 Place the two strips of fabric for the middle tier right sides together and pin both short ends. Stitch together to make one continuous strip of fabric, using a 1.5 cm (½ in) seam allowance. To make the bottom tier, place the three widths of fabric together at the short ends and stitch to make one continuous loop.

6 Fold the top tier fabric in half, match the edges together and pin. Machine-sew this seam using a 1.5 cm (½ in) seam allowance. Press the seams open and set aside.

7 On the top raw edge of the middle tier, starting 8–10 cm (3¼–4 in) from a seam, sew all the way around the tube using a longer stitch and leaving a 1.5 cm (½ in) seam allowance. Do NOT back stitch. Finish sewing exactly where you started. Pull the bobbin thread so the fabric starts to gather. Keep pulling until the gathered middle tier top edge is the same width as the circumference of the top tier.

Spread the gathering so it is even. With right sides together and side seams matching, pin the middle tier to the top tier, right sides together and raw edges aligned. Stitch the top and middle tiers together. Zigzag stitch along the raw edges to minimise fraying. Trim loose threads. Turn the layers right side out and topstitch around the top tier of fabric where the two tiers join.

8 Repeat the step to attach the bottom tier to the middle tier.

9 Turn in 5 mm (¼ in) at the top raw edge of the skirt and press, then turn in another 3 cm (1¼ in) and press. With the wrong side out, pin, then stitch the waistband casing, leaving a large gap for feeding the elastic through.

IO Measure the elastic to fit the child's waist, allowing a 2 cm (¾ in) overlap. On one side of the elastic mark each end with a pen so you know that the elastic is flat inside the casing. Put a safety pin in one end of the elastic and feed it through the casing. Make sure both ends have pen marks on the same side, then overlap the elastic ends and sew them together. Topstitch closed the gap in the waistband. Trim all threads.

II Turn in 5 mm (¼ in) at the hem of the skirt and press, then turn in 1 cm (³⁄₈ in) and press. With the wrong side of the fabric facing up, topstitch around the hem. Trim the loose threads.

IDEAS

You could hand or machine appliqué a piece of one of the skirt fabrics on a tee-shirt or singlet, to make a co-ordinating top. For girls, I love to cut small circles of different sizes and machine appliqué them in layers to look like a brooch.

Ballerina Dress–Up Skirt

You will need

1.5 m (1 yd 2 ft) of wide ribbon (grosgrain ribbon works well), for the waist tie

1 m (40 in) (generous yard) of each of 3 colours of tulle 2.4 m (2¾ yd) wide

Co-ordinating thread

For many little girls, twirling around in a tutu pretending to be a ballerina is part of their make-believe play. I made this tutu-style skirt, gathering a couple of layers of tulle and attaching it onto wide ribbon to tie around the waist like a wrap skirt. Tulle comes in different weights and qualities. Bridal tulle is fine and soft and wide. If you find tulle in colours you love but it is narrow, use the narrow part for length and buy two metres (2½ yards) from the roll to use for width. You can work with tulle in either direction.

This skirt will fit a 4-year-old. If you want smaller or larger, just adjust the waist and length measurements.

I Measure the child's waist and cut a piece of ribbon to that length. Put the rest of the ribbon aside until later.

2 Measure a 1.5 cm (½ in) seam allowance on each end of the waist ribbon and mark with a pin.

3 Fold the ribbon in half, mark the centre with a pin, then add a pin at the quarter-way point and the three-quarter-way point, so the ribbon is marked out evenly into 4 sections.

4 Arrange the first piece of tulle, 1 x 2.4 m (1 x 2¾ yd), on the floor. Cut the 1 m (40 in) edge in half to make two pieces 50 cm (40 in) wide. Arrange the first cut piece on the floor, and top with the second cut piece. Repeat with the remaining lengths of tulle until you have six layers stacked up. Pin them together along one of the cut edges. This will now be the waist edge.

5 Using a bright coloured thread so that you can see it easily, set the sewing machine to the longest straight stitch and stitch the layers together 1.5 cm (½ in) from the cut edge. This stitching will be hidden between two layers of ribbon so it will not be seen. Stitch a second row of basting stitches 1 cm (3/8 in) from the waist cut edge.

6 Pull the two threads to start gathering the tulle to fit the ribbon waistband and ensure the gathers are spread evenly.

7 Pin the gathered tulle to the waistband, leaving the seam allowances free. Pin the ribbon to the tulle so that the middle point of the tulle is pinned to the centre pin on the ribbon. Pin the quarter pin points to the tulle.

8 Set the sewing machine to a small zigzag stitch. Place the waist under the sewing machine foot with the ribbon facing up. Sew along the bottom edge of the ribbon to secure the tulle to the ribbon. Back stitch to secure the threads.

9 Trim away the excess tulle to prevent the waist from being bulky.

10 Fold over the 1.5 cm (½ in) seam allowance of ribbon on both ends and pin in place. Take the long ribbon and pin the centre point of one long edge to the centre of the waist ribbon on the wrong side. Continue to pin it on each side of the centre pin so it is securely attached to the waist ribbon. Set the sewing machine to a regular length straight stitch and sew along the ribbon edge, just below the zigzag stitching. Sew the full length of the waist ribbon and along each short end to totally encase the tulle between the two layers of ribbon.

II Trim all loose threads, then test the length and trim accordingly. Trim any excess ribbon from the tie ends. To prevent the cut ends from fraying turn in a double hem and straight stitch to hold the ends.

HINTS

You could make the skirt using just one colour of tulle.

Simple Drawstring Dress

This drawstring dress is so simple to make and very comfortable to wear. It works well when layered with tee-shirts and leggings. I like to find ways to make projects simple, so for this dress I used ready-made bias binding rather than making it myself.

You will need

Fabric, for the dress

Co-ordinating thread, for the dress

Bias binding, for binding the armholes and ties

Co-ordinating thread for the bias binding

I Cut out the front and back of the dress using the pattern pieces provided. Set the pieces aside.

2 From bias binding, cut the arm bindings and tie according to the pattern. Set aside for later (*see pattern in envelope at back of book*).

3 Arrange the back of the dress, right side up, on the work surface. Put the dress front right side down on top, matching raw edges. Pin the right side seam from the underarm to the hem and sew in place. Reinforce the start and end of the stitching with back stitches. Repeat on the other side of the dress.

4 Change the sewing machine to a zigzag stitch, or use an overlocker, and zigzag stitch down each side seam. Trim all threads.

5 Pin the armhole binding along each armhole with the broader edge underneath. Trim the binding to even up the ends. With the right side of the dress facing up, machine-sew along the edge of the binding about 2–3 mm (1/8 in) from the edge.

6 To make the casing for the tie, turn in 5 mm (¼ in) at the front top raw edge of the dress and press. Turn in another hem, 2 cm (¾ in) deep and press. Sew along this edge, close to the fold, to secure the casing. Repeat for the back of the dress. Trim all threads.

7 Turn in 5 mm (¼ in) at the hem of the dress and press. Turn in another 1 cm (3/8 in), press and pin in place. Sew with a straight stitch around the hem, beginning 5 cm (2 in) from the side seam. Trim the threads.

8 To make the dress tie, open the end of the binding, turn over the end by 1cm (½ in) and fold the binding closed. Holding the end together sew the binding closed along the edge. Sew all along the length of the binding, stopping 8 cm (3¼ in) from the opposite end, with the needle down. Open out the other end of the binding, turn in a small seam as before and fold the binding in place. Continue machine-sewing to the end of the binding. Trim all loose thread ends.

9 Attach a safety pin to one end of the tie. Thread it through the back casing then through the front casing. Make a bow with the tie on the shoulder.

Wrap Dress

You will need

Fabric, for the dress

Binding, for the edges and ties

Co-ordinating threads

This simple wrap dress can be made in a variety of fabrics for use at different times of the year. Make it in light florals for the summer months, or thicker denim for the winter, and layer it over tees and leggings. It's a style that older girls like to wear as much as toddlers.

I Cut one dress back and two dress front pieces (*see pattern in envelope at back of book*), flipping the front pattern to cut the second piece if you are cutting the fabric in a single layer. Or, place the pattern on a folded length of fabric and cut both at the same time.

2 Zigzag stitch the shoulders on the back and front pieces. Pin the fronts to the back at the shoulders, with right sides together, and then sew the seams with a 1 cm ($3/8$ in) seam allowance. Press the seams open.

3 If you want to match the binding to the dress then cut out binding from the dress fabric. You will need two lengths of binding for armhole trim, two ties, and one long binding for the neckline. Alternatively, purchase bias binding that co-ordinates or contrasts with the dress. All trims and ties are made from the binding.

4 Cut two lengths of binding slightly longer than the armhole and pin in place. Pin the narrower side of purchased binding on the right side of the fabric. Pin to the fabric and topstitch from the right side, being sure to catch all layers when stitching.

5 Measure and cut the binding tie for the left seam.

6 Match the left front and the back pieces together, then pin the side seam through to the hem. Sew 2 cm (¾ in) down the seam then insert the tie between the layers so that 1 cm (³/8 in) is caught in the side seam stitching and the rest of the tie is sitting to the left. Continue sewing to the hem. Zigzag along the cut edges of the fabric to tidy the seam.

7 Now match the right front to the back of the dress and pin the side seam through to the hem. Measure down 2 cm (¾ in) and arrange the tie on the fabric with the cut short edge of the tie lined up with the cut edge of the fabric. Sew the side seam all the way down to the hem. Zigzag along the cut edge of the fabric to tidy the seam.

8 Turn in a 1 cm (³/8 in) hem at the bottom of the dress and press, then turn in another 1.5 cm (½ in) and press. Topstitch around the hem and trim the threads.

9 Turn in 1 cm (³/8 in) seam on the right front dress and press, then fold another 1.5 cm (½ in) and press. Topstitch from the top down to the hem edge. Repeat on the left front of the dress.

10 Measure the binding for the neckband. Find the middle point of the binding and pin this to the centre back neck, then pin each way from here. This will ensure the tie ends are equal in length. The ties are not very long. If you want to tie them into a bow add

some extra to the bindings. Fold the cut end of the binding inside and fold the binding closed and pin. Repeat on the other end. Now topstitch from one end of a tie up the front of the dress and down the other side to the end of the other tie.

NOTE

The two front panels have binding along the edges. One side seam has a short binding tie on the outside, the other side seam has a short binding tie on the inside. Two short ties (12– 15 cm (4¾–6 in) long): one goes inside on a side seam and one outside on the other side seam. Then the binding for the front edges and around the neck band have long ends to tie onto the two short ties, one inside the dress and the other outside the dress.

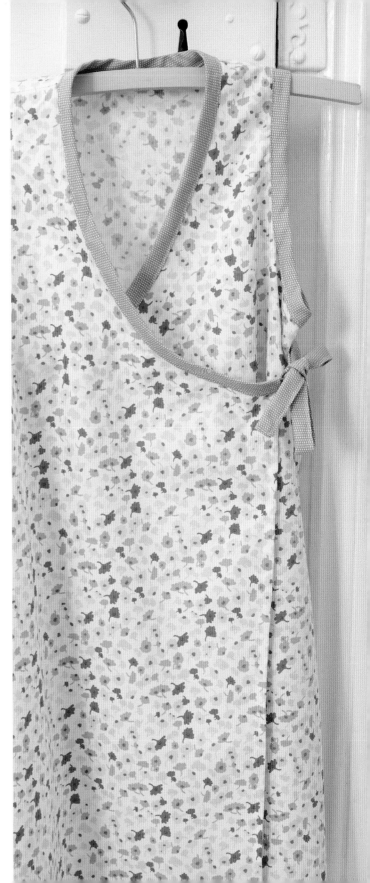

Headband

This double-sided fabric headband is easy to make and works brilliantly. Use up fabric offcuts from other projects. It makes a cute present.

I Using the pattern template provided, cut out two pieces of fabric on the fold (from the same or different fabrics). Press the fabric.

2 Cut out one piece of fusible interfacing using the pattern as a guide.

3 Iron the fusible interfacing to the back of one piece of headband fabric.

4 On both pieces of fabric fold the narrow ends of the fabric over by half and press (as marked on the pattern).

5 Arrange the piece of fabric without interfacing right side up. Place the second piece of fabric right side down on top (with the interfacing on top).

6 With a 6–7 mm (¼ in) seam allowance, machine-stitch down one long side. Cut the threads then repeat down the other side to make one piece.

You will need

Headband template (see p. 127)

Two pieces of cotton fabric, 40 x 8 cm (16 x 3¼ in)

15 cm (6 in) length of 1 cm (³⁄₈ in) wide elastic

Piece of lightweight fusible interfacing, 35 x 8 cm (13¾ x 3¼ in)

Co-ordinating thread

7 Trim the excess seam allowance fabric, close to the stitching.

8 Turn the headband right side out and press flat.

9 Take one end of the elastic and insert about 1 cm (³/₈ in) inside an open end of the headband. Topstitch across the elastic twice to secure, then continue down the side of the headband about 5 mm (¼ in) in from the edge. When you get to the other open end insert the other end of the elastic (taking care not to twist it) about 1 cm (³/₈ in) inside the end and stitch over twice to secure. Continue topstitching along the other side to where you began. Back stitch a few stitches and cut threads.

HINTS

You can make headbands to co-ordinate or match other clothes.

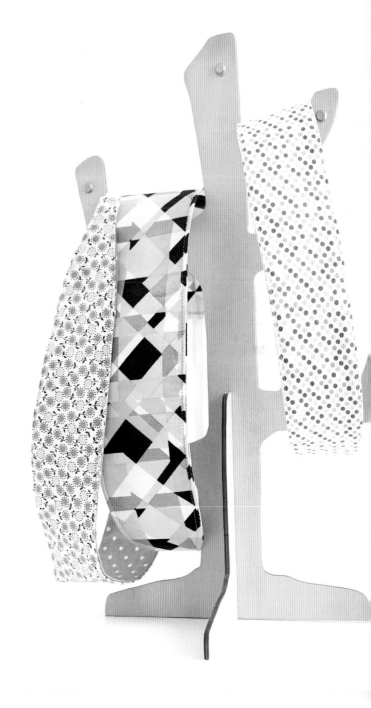

Girl's Summer Top

Soft flowing cotton feels so cool against the skin and looks smarter than a tee-shirt. This simple top is a classic shape and easy to wear. It is pulled over the head, with no buttons or fuss. Makes for easy sewing too.

You will need

Cotton fabric

Elastic for neckband (5 mm/¼ in width)

Co-ordinating thread

I Cut out the front, back and two sleeves using the pattern provided (*see pattern in envelope*).

2 Turn in a 5 mm (¼ in) hem on the sleeve edges and press, then turn in another 5 mm (¼ in), press and pin. Topstitch in place. Repeat on the other sleeve.

3 Match the shoulder seams on the right side and sew the front to the back with a 1 cm (³/8 in) seam allowance. Repeat for the left-side shoulder seam.

4 With right sides together, pin a sleeve into place. Sew the sleeve into position with a 1 cm (³/8 in) seam allowance. Zigzag stitch over the seam. Repeat for the other sleeve.

5 Match and pin the side seams from the underarm to the hem, then sew in place. Repeat on the other side.

6 Turn the underarm edge over by 5 mm (¼ in) and topstitch in place.

7 Fold in a 5 mm (¼ in) hem at the waist and press, then fold in another 1 cm (³/₈ in), press and pin. Topstitch around with wrong side of the fabric facing up. Start on the back near a side seam to make it less noticeable. Secure the stitching with some back stitches.

8 Fold in the neck edge by 5 mm (¼ in) and press, then 1 cm (³/₈ in) press and pin. With the wrong side facing up, stitch along the edge, topstitch along the edge to make the casing for the elastic. Be sure to leave a small gap towards the back to feed the elastic through.

9 Attach a safety pin to the end of the elastic and feed it through. Machine-sew the ends of the elastic together to secure, then topstitch the gap closed. Trim the threads.

Simple Patching

You will need

Fabric patch large enough to cover the problem area

Appliqué paper (fusible webbing)

Co-ordinating thread

Kids can be tough on clothes. Accidents happen and the knees of trousers, for example, get torn or holes appear in odd places in garments. Rather than discarding them why not make some funky patches? If the damage is in an area that receives plenty of wear and tear such as the knee or backside, choose a fabric patch that is robust. If the area to be patched is very small, such as on narrow legs, it can be tricky to manoeuvre the garment under the needle of your machine. You can always do some fun hand-stitching to secure the patch.

There are two ways to add the fabric patch. You could cut a patch, then sew it in place around the edges with a straight stitch (the edges will fray a little in the wash). You could use a zigzag stitch, which would hold the edge of the fabric a little more and minimise fraying. The second way is to turn in the raw edges of the fabric on the patch.

I Cut a piece of patching fabric large enough to cover the hole or rip with some overlap. If you want to fold

under the edges for a neat square or rectangular patch ensure you cut a piece large enough so that when you sew it in place you are stitching into the garment where the fabric is sound.

2 Place the patch wrong side up on the ironing board. Cut a piece of appliqué paper to the size of the fabric. Protecting the iron and ironing board, iron the appliqué paper onto the fabric patch and set aside for about 30 minutes to cool.

3 Peel the backing paper off the patch, position over the hole and adhere to the garment by rubbing over with a hot iron.

4 To secure the patch, sew around the outline, a few millimetres in from the edge with a straight stitch. For the rough-cut patch you could use a zigzag stitch, capturing the edge of the fabric to minimise fraying. Trim all ends.

HINTS

If the hole is quite large do not use the appliqué paper; simply pin the patch in place and sew. The appliqué paper works best on small holes, tears or when fabric is worn thin but still holding together.

If the bottom of the legs are worn, use bias binding to cover the frayed edge. If you don't have a bias binding that suits you could make some. It doesn't need to be cut on the bias.

On denim jeans I often patch with another scrap of denim in a similar colour or flip the denim patch over and put the back of the denim on the outside to add some interest to the patch.

Boy's Shorts

Kids favour clothes that are easy to put on and are comfortable to wear. A pair of shorts with a tee-shirt is a favourite way for little boys to dress through the summer months. This pattern will work for girls too. You can adjust the leg length and the width of the waist elastic to suit the child you are making for.

You will need

3 cm (1¼ in) wide non-roll elastic (cut slightly shorter than waist measurement)

Fabric, for the shorts

Co-ordinated thread

1 Place the pattern pieces (*see pattern in envelope at back of book*) on two layers of fabric with right sides facing. Cut out 2 fronts and 2 backs. Clearly mark the front and back of the shorts with a fading marker pen to prevent any confusion.

2 Measure the child's waist and cut the elastic just a little shorter than the waist measurement so that the elastic is stretched a little when the shorts are worn, keeping them in place. Set the elastic aside.

3 Take the right front and the right back and pin along the outside leg seam. Sew the side seam, then zigzag the seam allowance together and press to the back. Repeat for the left leg.

4 Match the inside leg seams and pin together. Stitch the inside leg seams and then zigzag the seam allowance together and press to the back.

5 To sew the crotch seam, turn one of the legs right side out. Put the right-side out fabric leg inside the other and match up and pin the crotch seam. Sew this seam, then zigzag stitch along the cut edge to tidy the seam. Push the seam allowance to the back and reinforce the crotch with an 8 cm (3¼ in) line of stitching between the zigzag stitches and the seam, sewing through the two layers of seam allowance and the back left and right side fabric.

6 Fold the waistband over by 1 cm (³/8 in) and press, then over again by 3.5 cm (1½ in) and press. Topstitch the waistband in place to make a casing for the elastic, leaving a 3 cm (1¼ in) gap in the seam to feed the elastic through.

7 With a pen, mark each end of the elastic on the same side. Attach a safety pin to the elastic and feed it through the gap on the waistband.

Once the elastic is through check that the pen marks are facing in the same direction so you know you haven't twisted the elastic inside the casing. Join the two ends securely on your sewing machine. Topstitch the elastic gap closed.

8 To hem the bottom of the shorts, turn in the hem by 1.5 cm (½ in) and press, then turn in another 1.5 cm (½ in) and stitch in place.

HINTS

Try the shorts on the child before you hem them. If they are too long trim the length. Lengthen or reduce the leg length depending on your preference.

Girls prefer narrow waist elastic, such as 2 cm (¾ in) or 2.5 cm (1 in) wide. Just adjust the fabric at the top of the pattern to suit your elastic width.

Pyjama Pants

These comfortable pyjama pants can be made in fine cotton or soft flannelette.

1 Arrange the pattern pieces (*see pattern in envelope at back of book*) on the fabric and cut out. If you are cutting from a single layer of fabric remember to flip the pattern pieces to cut one right and one left piece.

2 With a fading marker pen, clearly mark the front and back pieces.

3 Pin the back right and front right-hand sides together down the outside leg. Sew the side seams. Change to zigzag stitch and sew over the seam allowance to hold the fabric edges. Press the seams to the back. Repeat for the left leg.

4 Match up the inside leg seams, pin together, then sew the seam. Zigzag along the seam allowance. Press to the back.

5 To sew the crotch seam turn one leg right-side out then put it inside the other leg with outside leg seams together. Match the pieces, pin, then stitch in place. Push the seam

You will need

Fabric

2 cm (¾ in) non-roll elastic for waist

Co-ordinated thread

allowance to one side and reinforce the crotch with an 8 cm (3¼ in) line of stitching between the zigzag stitches and the seam, sewing through the two layers of seam allowance and the back left and right-side fabric.

6 Cut the elastic a little shorter than the waist measurement.

7 Fold the waistband over by 1 cm (³/8 in) and press, then over again by 3.5 cm (1½ in) and press. Topstitch the waistband to make a casing to feed the elastic through, leaving a 3 cm (1¼ in) gap at the back near the side seams. With a pen, mark each end of the elastic on the same side. Attach a safety pin to the elastic and feed it through the gap, making sure the pen marks are still facing the same direction. Stitch the elastic ends securely. Topstitch the gap closed on the machine.

8 Hem the bottom of the pyjama legs. Turn the fabric over by 1 cm (³/8 in), press, then turn again by 1 cm (³/8 in) and topstitch in place.

HINTS

Try the pyjamas pants on the child to check the length before sewing the hem.

Boys may prefer wider elastic in the waist. Remember to add the extra width to the depth of the waistband when cutting out the fabric.

For pattern size 2, the hem at the bottom of legs (step 8) is too narrow to machine hem once the inside leg seam is sewn.

Machine-Appliquéd Tee-Shirt

You will need

Tee-shirt

Fabric, for the motif

Appliqué paper (fusible webbing)

Co-ordinating thread

Machine appliqué is used to decorate an individual tee for a boy. The machine stitching can be either a straight stitch sewn a few millimetres in from the raw edge of the fabric, which will soften and fray a little when washed, or a close zigzag stitch over the cut edge of the fabric. For the appliqué shape, either find material with a motif that you can cut out, such as one with rockets on it and cut out around the shape, or find a shape such as a duck, or even a big circle in an art stencil or kid's book and trace it, then transfer the tracing onto appliqué paper. Make sure the shape is easy to sew around.

1 If you are picking out a motif from a fabric, cut a piece of appliqué paper slightly larger than the design.

2 If you are using a template, cut enough fabric and appliqué paper to fit the shape. Trace the reverse image of the shape onto the appliqué paper.

3 Iron the appliqué paper to the wrong side of the appliqué fabric. Using sharp scissors cut out around the design or shape. Set aside to cool. When cold, peel off the backing paper.

4 Place the tee-shirt on the ironing board, position the fabric shape and gently rub over it with a hot iron.

5 Machine-stitch (straight or zigzag) to secure the fabric in place. Sew around to the starting point and overlap by a few stitches and fasten off at the back of the work.

Apron

You will need

Fabric, for the apron

2 m (2 yd 6 in) bias binding for the neckband and ties. (Exact length required depends on the apron size)

Co-ordinating thread

Kids love to help in the kitchen and invariably become messy. Protect their clothes with these colourful aprons. They are simple to make, with or without a pocket, depending on time and fabric. Some kids love a pocket; others fill it with sticky beaten egg or breadcrumbs, so I will leave it to you to decide. The pattern for this is in the envelope at the back of the book.

I Cut out the fabric for the apron to the required size. If you want to add a pocket cut one from fabric.

2 Turn over the top cut edge of the bodice by 5 mm (¼ in) and press, then over by 1 cm (³/₈ in) and press. Topstitch this seam.

3 If you want to add a pocket do so next. Turn over the top edge by 5 mm (¼ in) and press, then over by 1 cm (³/₈ in) and press. Stitch along the folded edge. Zigzag stitch along the bottom cut edge, then turn under 1 cm (³/₈ in) and press.

4 Arrange the apron right side up and position the pocket right side up

on top. Pin in position. Sew down one side, along the bottom and up the other side of the pocket. Trim the thread ends.

5 Turn in 5 mm (¼ in) hems down both sides of the apron and press, then turn in another 1 cm (³/8 in) and press. Topstitch the seams.

6 Turn in the hem by 5 mm (¼ in) and press, then 1 cm (³/8 in), press and sew.

7 Measure 45 cm (17¾ in) of binding and mark with a pin. This is a waistband tie. Align the pin with the bottom of the sloping edge of the apron bodice, ensuring that the narrow edge of the binding is face up. Pin the sloping edge of the bodice between the fold of the bias binding, encasing the sloping edge of the apron. Measure and mark with a pin another 45 cm (17¾ in) and align the pin with the top of the sloping bodice at the opposite side. The bias binding forms the neckband of the apron. Encase the sloping edge in the binding as before, finishing at the bottom of the sloping edge. The rest of the binding forms the other waistband tie. Make sure the two ties are of equal length. Open out the binding at each end of the tie, turn in a small hem and refold.

8 Starting on the left-hand side of the binding, sew along the tie, up the side of the apron, around the neckband, down the other side of the apron and through to the end of the tie. Trim any loose threads.

HINT

I recommend cotton drill for this project, which is a medium-weight cotton fabric, and offers good protection for your kids' clothes.

Going Out

Small Purse

Kids of all ages love to put treasured objects into a purse for taking shopping, to school or just on outings. This project is perfect to use up some offcuts and makes a useful gift. I often make one then pop a small something inside.

You will need

2 pieces denim or medium-weight fabric for the purse, 22 x 16.5 cm (8½ x 6½ in)

Co-ordinated zipper 18 cm (8½ in) long

Co-ordinating threads

1 Zigzag stitch along both top edges of the purse front and back where the zipper will go, remembering to do a few back stitches to secure the seams and prevent fraying.

2 With the wrong side of the fabric up, turn the top long edge in by 1 cm (³/8 in) and press. Repeat on the other piece of fabric.

3 Pin the zipper into place with the folded and pressed top edges of the purse as close to the zipper teeth as you can.

4 Sew down each side of the zipper, using the zipper foot attachment, about 3 mm (¹/8 in) from the teeth.

5 Open the zipper about half way to make it possible to turn the purse right way out after sewing. Pin the two pieces of purse right sides together

with a 1 cm (^{3}/$_8$ in) seam allowance. Starting at the top right corner, machine straight stitch down one side, along the bottom and up the other side. Change your sewing machine to a zigzag stitch and machine around the three edges to catch the cut edges of the fabric and to minimise fraying. Trim all loose threads.

7 Turn the purse right side out. Use the point of your scissors to push out the corners.

HINTS

You can vary the size for different ages or for different uses. This project could easily be turned into a pencil case, but remember to select an appropriate fabric.

You could topstitch on a fabric stripe, ric-rac or ribbon trim on the front of the purse.

Zipper ends can be a bit tricky. It can get bulky at the side seams with fabric layers and zipper ends. If you have positioned the zipper correctly and machined up the sides in the right place it should turn right way out with neat ends. If you need to you can always do a few hand stitches in a co-ordinating colour to resolve any problems. The more zippers you insert the more confident you will become.

Small Shoulder Bag

You will need

Two pieces of fabric, 25 x 22 cm (10 x 8½ in)

1.2 m (47 in) cotton webbing strap, 2.5 cm (1 in) wide

18 cm (7 in) zipper, to match bag fabric

Contrast fabric for stripe on the front, 22 x 7 cm (8½ x 2¾ in)

Co-ordinating thread

Fray stopper liquid (optional)

Little girls reach an age where they want to be just like mum and have a handbag. On outings they need to carry the essentials of life – electronic games and pocket money. This style, held across the body, stops the strap constantly sliding off the shoulder.

I like to make the bag with a denim chambray or cotton drill as both are robust fabrics. You can add contrast fabric to the front of the bag for decoration or even a strip of ribbon or ric-rac. Play around with scraps and individualise the bags you make. For the strap, I use navy blue cotton webbing but you could use a contrast colour, if you wish.

I Zigzag stitch along one of the short edges on the front and back fabrics of the bag. These two edges will be the top of the bag where the zipper will be fitted. Set aside.

2 Take the contrast fabric for the front of the bag and turn in 1 cm (³/8 in) on the long sides of the contrast fabric and press.

3 Place the pressed contrast fabric piece on the right side of the front

fabric of the bag. The bottom of the contrast fabric should be 8 cm (3¼ in) from the bottom edge of the bag. Pin in place and topstitch to secure.

4 Zigzag stitch across the raw ends of the shoulder strap webbing to minimise fraying. Use fray stopper, if you like.

5 Place the back fabric of the bag right side up on the work table so the zigzag-stitched short edge is at the top. Pin a cut end of the webbing strap 2 cm (¾ in) in from the side edge and pin in place so that 5 mm (¼ in) of the webbing overhangs the top edge of the bag. Repeat this step with the other cut end of the webbing strap on the other side. Make sure there is no twist in the strap. Using a straight machine stitch, secure the straps to the bag about 5 mm (¼ in) from the edge.

6 Turn the top edges of the front and back of the bag in by 1 cm (³/8 in) and press.

7 Check the zipper works properly before you sew it in place. Pin the zipper into place with the folded and

pressed top edges of the bag as close to the zipper teeth as possible. Using the zipper foot, sew the front of the bag to the zipper first, as close to the zipper teeth as you can. Then sew down the other side, securing the back of the bag to the zipper, as close to the zipper teeth as you can. As you sew this seam the strap will be to your left-hand side.

8 Open the zipper about half way, then pin the front and back of the bag facing right sides together with a 1 cm (3/8 in) seam allowance. Be sure to have the strap inside the bag and out of the way of the side seams. Starting at the top right corner, sew down one side, along the bottom and up the other side. Zigzag stitch around the three sides to catch the raw edges of the fabric. Trim all loose threads.

9 Turn the bag right side out and push out the corners.

HINT

The ends of the zipper can be tricky. It can get a little bulky with the side seams and the zipper ends. To get the idea of spacing required, pin the zipper in place and hold the side seams as if they were sewn, and see how the zipper fits.

If you have positioned the zipper correctly and machined up the sides in the right place it should turn right way out with neat ends. If you need to you can always do a few hand stitches in a co-ordinating colour to resolve any tiny problems. I prefer to match the zipper to the fabric then any glitches are less noticeable.

Tote Bag

You will need

Medium-weight fabric, for the bag, 90 x 45 cm (35½ x 17¾ in)

Fabric, for the straps, 68 x 20 cm (26¾ x 8 in)

Co-ordinating thread

Tote bags are useful to have, especially now we're all trying to reduce our use of plastic carrier bags. They're stylish too. Keep one in the car and one folded up in the bottom of your handbag and you will be ready to haul the shopping home anytime.

The best fabric for a tote bag is a medium-weight cotton. Quilting cotton is too light but cotton drill or light cotton canvas will make a strong bag. You could also use upholstery fabric.

This project uses a French seam to join the bag together. French seams are strong and neat. There is an explanation of how to sew a French seam on page 8. Practise with offcuts before working on your bag.

I Cut a bag front and a bag back, each 45 cm (17¾ in) square. Cut two shoulder straps, 68 x 10 cm (26¾ x 4 in).

2 Pin the bag front and back wrong sides together. Allowing a 5 mm (¼ in) seam allowance and starting at the top of one side, sew around three edges. Clip off the corners to reduce bulk.

3 Turn the bag wrong sides out. Allowing a 1 cm (³/₈ in) seam allowance, sew around the three edges. This is a French seam, encasing the raw edges of the fabric within a seam. It is very strong and gives a neat finish.

4 To box the bottom corners of the bag, fold a corner into a point so the side seam is centred at the apex and in line with the bottom seam. Measure 5 cm (2 in) down the seam from the apex and rule a line across the corner. Sew along the ruled line, being sure to back stitch when beginning and ending to secure the stitching. It is a good idea to sew a second line of stitching on the corner side of the first line of stitching for extra strength. Do not trim off the corner of fabric. Repeat for the other corner.

5 Fold in 1 cm (³/₈ in) at the top raw edge of the bag and press with an iron. Turn in another 1 cm (³/₈ in) and press again. Topstitch as close as possible to the inner folded edge. Turn the bag right side out and set aside.

6 With right sides together, fold each strap in half lengthwise. Leaving a 1 cm (³/₈ in) seam allowance, sew along the length of the straps leaving both short ends open. Turn the fabric straps right side out.

7 Press the tube of fabric so that the seam is centred on one side. Fold in 1 cm (³/₈ in) at the short ends of the strap and press. If you like, topstitch along each edge of the strap, sewing 3 mm (¹/₈ in) in from the edge of the fabric. Otherwise, topstitch each short end.

8 To position the first strap, measure 7 cm (2¾ in) from the side seam of the bag and mark the spot with a pin on the outside of the bag. Line up the outside edge of the strap against the pin marker and pin in place. Position the strap so that 4 cm (1½ in) of strap will be attached to the bag. Remember the seam side of the strap faces the right side of the bag fabric. Stitch the strap onto the bag by sewing a square then intersecting diagonal lines through the square for extra strength. Repeat on the same

side of the bag for the other end of the strap. Turn the bag over and attach the second strap. Press the bag.

Muslin Baby Wrap

A muslin light wrap is very useful when heading out and about with a baby in the warmer months. Even in warm weather small babies still need to be swaddled or wrapped tightly and a large muslin wrap is ideal. Add some beautiful binding to the edge and it is not only practical but unique. Makes a thoughtful present for a new arrival too.

You will need

Large plain muslin wrap (store bought) or a large square of muslin about 1.2 m x 1.2 m (48 x 48 in)

5 m (5½ yd) co-ordinating bias binding

Co-ordinating thread

I If you are using fabric bought off a roll, ensure the piece is square.

2 Pin the bias binding around the edge of the fabric or wrap. Begin about 15 cm (6 in) from a corner. Pin along to a corner then make a pleat, creating a simplified mitred corner. Continue pinning along the next edge, next corner and so on until you are about 10 cm (4 in) from the starting point. Fold under the loose end of the bias binding so that when you sew to the end it will be a neat finish.

3 Sew around the binding a few millimetres in from the inside edge and being sure to back stitch at the beginning and end to secure the stitching. Trim all loose threads.

HINTS

The first time I sewed binding around the folded corners the fabric seemed to slip, making sewing it in place very tricky. The next time I tackled sewing binding around a square corner I hand-tacked around the corners with big stitches in bright contrasting thread to hold the fabric in place. Then I machine-stitched around the square and the corners were much easier to manage. Once the binding is secure, use a seam ripper to take out the basting stitches.

This would also work well with a soft flannelette wrap for winter baby presents. Keep the wrap generous and square for easy baby swaddling.

Templates

Heart Template

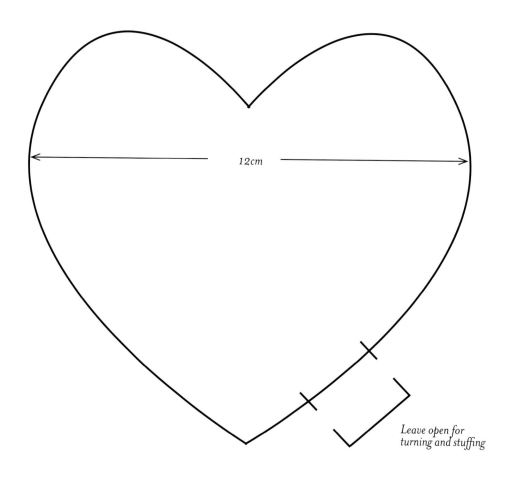

12cm

Leave open for turning and stuffing

Bunting Template

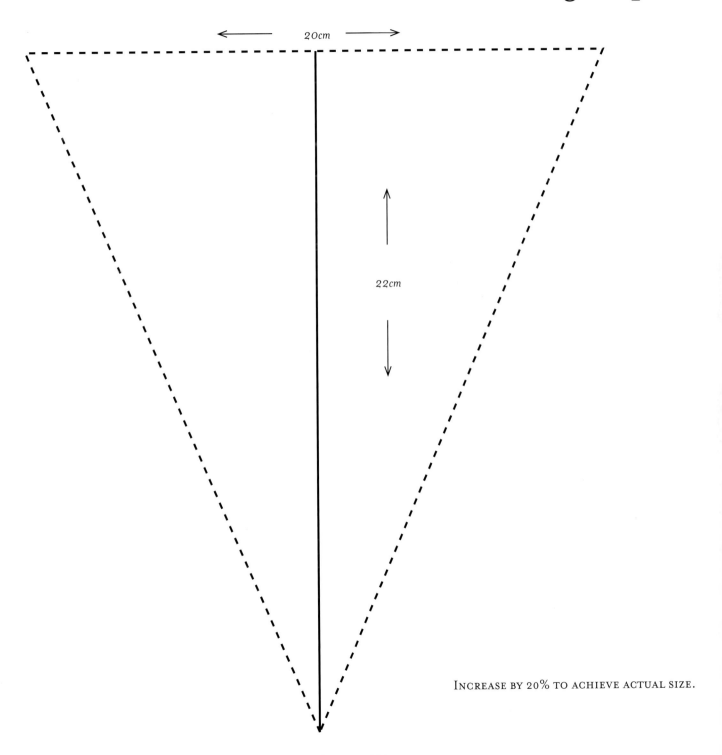

20cm

22cm

INCREASE BY 20% TO ACHIEVE ACTUAL SIZE.

Owl Template

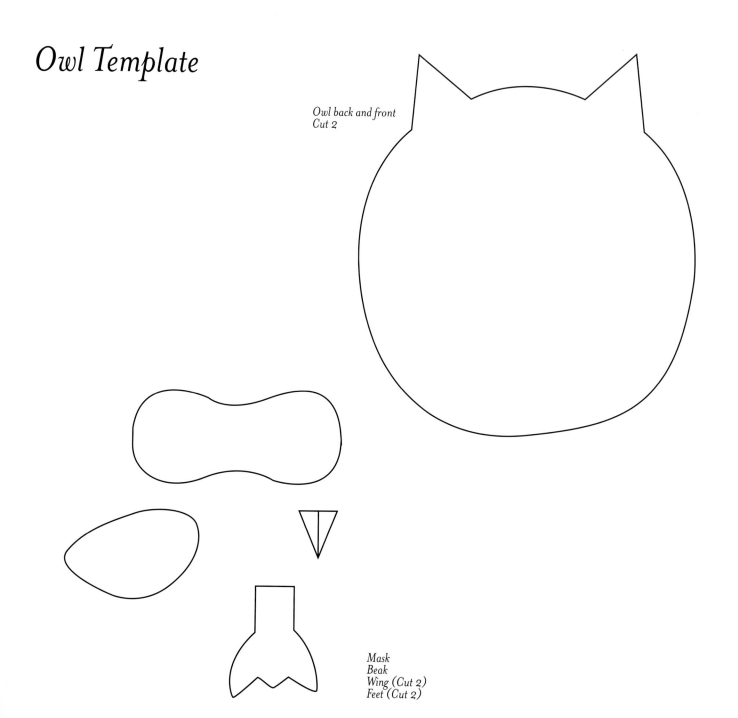

*Owl back and front
Cut 2*

*Mask
Beak
Wing (Cut 2)
Feet (Cut 2)*

<small>INCREASE BY 50% TO ACHIEVE ACTUAL SIZE.</small>

Opening for turning and stuffing

How to pin before sewing a front and back together. Pins must be at the back.

INCREASE BY 80% TO ACHIEVE ACTUAL SIZE.

Appliquéd Baby Singlet Template

INCREASE BY 80% TO ACHIEVE ACTUAL SIZE.

Headband Template

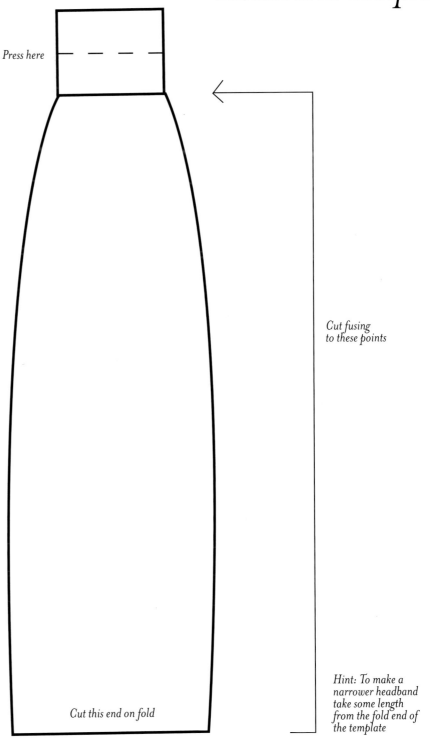

Press here

Cut fusing to these points

Hint: To make a narrower headband take some length from the fold end of the template

ACTUAL SIZE

Cut this end on fold

Index